HABITS FOR SUCCESS

sound
wisdom.
Because Your Success Matters

SOUND WISDOM BOOKS
BY EARL NIGHTINGALE

THE STRANGEST SECRET SERIES

Quit thinking about your losses...get yourself into a positive frame of mind.

—NAPOLEON HILL'S
GUIDE TO ACHIEVING YOUR GOALS

EARL NIGHTINGALE
HABITS FOR SUCCESS

The Pathway to Self-Mastery and Freedom

THE STRANGEST SECRET SERIES

Published and distributed by:
SOUND WISDOM
P.O. Box 310
Shippensburg, PA 17257-0310
717-530-2122

info@soundwisdom.com

www.soundwisdom.com

ISBN 13 TP: 978-1-64095-509-7

ISBN 13 eBook: 978-1-64095-510-3

For Worldwide Distribution, Printed in the U.S.A.

1 2 3 4 5 6 7 8 / 29 28 27 26 25

The only limits to your accomplishments in life are self-imposed.

—DENIS WAITLEY,
THE PSYCHOLOGY OF WINNING

CONTENTS

INTRODUCTION

by Vic Conant

My dad, Lloyd Conant, met Earl Nightingale in 1956 when Earl was a popular radio commentator on WGN in Chicago. At the time, Dad was a successful businessman—he owned his own direct marketing and printing company. Earl had just produced a recording titled *The Strangest Secret* and was looking for someone to market that product. The two of them met and Dad ended up selling a million of that recording over the years. These two men were a match made in Heaven. My dad the marketer and Earl the talent.

Earl, like Lloyd, was a "Great Depression" era child and grew up poor in California. Earl educated himself; he was an avid reader and a brilliant guy. Both had only a high school education. Earl was a totally self-made man as was my dad, so the two of them hit it off and eventually created Nightingale-Conant when I was about 14.

Every individual who has discovered what Earl Nightingale calls *The Strangest Secret* throughout the ages has found it to be a profoundly life-changing discovery. That secret? *You become what you think about*—and the fact that our thoughts *control,* and many believe, *create* our reality. Consequently, there is great responsibility placed on our thinking, making us responsible for our own future.

Vic Conant
Chairman of the Board
Nightingale-Conant Corporation

1

FOR THE BETTER

*"The secret of happiness is freedom
and the secret of freedom, courage."*

—Pericles,

Greek cultural and political leader

One of the most interesting things about people is that
they can and do change for the better. A person who was
once a criminal becomes a model citizen. Another person
kicks a drug habit and begins living a life of responsibility
and contribution. And for every one of those there are millions who over a span of years have become substantially
better as persons, who are kinder, more honest, more conscientious about their responsibilities, and so on. But just
how does a person improve and why?

To be your best is an act of will. Actions completed
every day over a period of time create competence that will
take you to the top. Daily actions become habits. There are
good habits and there are bad habits. However, breaking

a bad habit and replacing it with productive good habits is necessary if you are to earn what you're worth.

In his Strictly Personal *Chicago Daily News* column, Sydney J. Harris wrote:

> It is not an act of intellect that makes people change themselves for the better. Not a matter of insight, but an act of the will. For intelligence without courage is as static as courage without intelligence is rash. It is not an act of intellect that makes people change themselves for the better, but an act of the will. For intelligence without courage is as static as courage without intelligence is rash. It is intelligence with courage that results in the necessary act of the will we need in order to bring about constructive change in ourselves.
>
> The person who breaks a bad and destructive habit does so by an act of the will. His intelligence tells him that he has a bad habit. It may be a work habit. It may be a steady habit or a non-steady habit. It might be a drug habit. It can be any sort of non-productive or destructive habit. Any person with a bad habit knows about it. His intelligence informs him.
>
> But changing a bad habit into a good one or at least getting rid of the bad one takes an act of the will over a sufficiently long period of time

to render it impotent. After a period of time, a surprisingly short time for most habits, it no longer clamors for attention. It fades away and finally disappears. Now the will can be turned off. The habit is gone. But it is turning on the will to undertake such a task that takes courage.

When we rid ourselves of unproductive and debilitating habits, we literally free ourselves to that degree. The more bad habits we can get rid of, the freer we become, the happier we become, the better our self-image becomes. The secret of happiness is freedom, but the secret of freedom, courage. "For intelligence without courage," as Syd Harris wrote, "is as static as courage without intelligence is rash."

Habits that make us happy we should keep. Habits that lead to unhappiness and illness we should try to muster the courage to end. It's surprising how easily a bad habit is routed once it's faced with courage. As Emerson said, "What a new face courage puts on everything."

True competency is built on habitual courage. It takes courage to make big plans. I recommend that you make no little plans. There's nothing in little plans to stir people's blood. Make big plans. Once a big idea is recorded, it can never die.

How big are your plans? If you're finding your daily life something of a bore or rather humdrum or uninteresting, it could be because your plans are too small. More people

True competency
is built on
habitual courage.

would make bigger plans if they knew they could be accomplished. The men who have stood out in history have been those with big plans that caught the fancy and imagination of others.

Even a family with a big plan toward which they're working is a happy, busy, and interesting family. There's less boredom and they have no time for bickering or looking for convenient means of escape.

You might, just for fun, stop a minute and reevaluate your plans. What are they? What are you working toward? Is it big enough for you? Does it fill you with excitement when you think about it, and does it fill your days with energy and accomplishment? If not, maybe your plans are too small. Maybe you're trying to play it safe with your one chance at life here on Earth.

All too often there's a wide gap between what a person started out to accomplish and what they have actually accomplished. Usually, there are very good reasons for your wanting to accomplish a particular thing. It's usually your particular talents and abilities trying to get you on the course that's right for you. You are unique—unlike any person who ever appeared on earth, but are you acting like other people? There's no good reason to do that. What is it that you want to do or have more than anything else? If you can answer that question, you can discover the direction you should very probably take.

People accomplish what they set out to accomplish, but they often don't realize the extent of their own greatness, and make their plans accordingly. They take their cue from those around them, assuming that what others do is right for them also. Maybe it is, but maybe it isn't. Of one thing you can be sure. If the plan you're working toward does not keep you interested and fill you with excitement at the prospect of its accomplishment, your plan is probably too small.

What do you really want to do? Why don't you do it? If it's good and hurts no one, go after it. You might be amazed at what you can do—people usually are when they discover that the goals that come naturally to them do so for very good reasons. No one will really desire with all their heart something that is beyond their accomplishment.

2

DEEP RESERVOIRS OF ABILITY

"Successful and competent people know how to admire others for their strengths."

—Earl Nightingale

Experts say that each of us has deep reservoirs of ability, even genius, that we habitually fail to make use of. We fail to make use of our own private and individual talents, because we're caught up in the absurd and impossible game of trying to be like other people who could no more be like us than we could be like them. We forget that other people feel inferior too. Since there's no one else on earth just like us, how can we be inferior? We are each one of a kind, defying rigid comparison by any measuring stick.

Well-adjusted people frankly admire others for their talents and abilities without feeling envious. In fact, they don't even bring themselves into comparison at all. They're happily resigned to the fact that they're not the

You can't lose money on a customer if you treat people the way they should be treated.

best-looking, best-built, smartest, most-talented, fastest, cleverest, funniest, most-engaging people on earth. Without even thinking about it, they seem to know that every person is a potpourri of strengths and weaknesses inherited from all their ancestors. No two were alike—each had a slightly different strong point with the standard collection of weaknesses.

If we have knobby knees, or big feet, or an off-kilter figure, or have to wear glasses, or fail to be as loveable or can't do complicated mathematical equations in our heads, we still represent what we've been given. The most intelligent and healthy attitude we can have is to make best use of what we do have, and what we have is considerable. Successful and competent people know how to admire others for their strengths.

If you want to make it on your own in your own organization, and most entrepreneurs do, then you must become a people person, whether you like the idea or not. You have two audiences that must like you and feel you have their interests in heart. One, your customers and prospects, and two, your employees. People do matter. People make all the difference in the world; and if they're not with you, you go out of business.

You are serving people in some capacity—and it's people you depend on for part of the money they earn each month. They will happily share their financial resources with you if you give them good service, if they feel important in your place of business or using your product or service.

They don't care about business school numbers. They're like flowers. They turn their faces and open their wallets and purses to the radiance of people who love and respect them enough to do business their way.

People will make you rich or keep you broke, depending on the way you serve them. If you're planning to become a successful entrepreneur, you should make up your mind at the outset to make people your special concern, which includes people outside the organization and those within the organization. You can't lose money on a customer if you treat him or her the way they should be treated.

Famous Chicago department store owner Marshall Field received a lot of kidding because of his policy to allow merchandise to be returned if the buyer was not completely satisfied. Women used to pretend to buy expensive fur coats, wear them for an important occasion, then return them for a full credit the following day. But when kidded about such things, Marshall Field used to request that the woman's account be sent up to show to his criticizing friend. Without fail, the woman was a good regular customer who bought many other things on her account. She was a good customer, and if she wanted to borrow a mink coat for an evening, so what? Chances are she'd talk her husband into buying one for her eventually. If not, she was still a good customer. It was his treatment of the customer that was largely responsible for Marshall Field's outstanding success.

It's the same story at Neiman Marcus and other high-end, successful stores. The customer deserves respect, always. There's never an excuse on the part of management for a customer being mistreated in any way. It simply shows a lack of training, and the lack of training of employees is one of the greatest problems of American business. Not giving recognition to the customer is the worst offense anyone in business can commit.

To see daily success and forward momentum, establish the habit of a friendly and respectful attitude to not only customers but everyone with whom you interact.

3

WHAT PEOPLE WANT

"Don't make your customers wait."

—Earl Nightingale

Recognition is number one on the hierarchy of human wants. People want to be recognized. Stimulation or change is number two, and security is number three. The good businessperson and each employee, because of their training, can give the customer all three of those.

The customer should be recognized if at all possible when he or she enters the place of business. If the customer has to wait in line, special attention should be given to those waiting, even a glance and the words, "I'll be with you as soon as I can," gives the required recognition. And no customer should ever leave a business, a gas station, convenience store, restaurant, or any other sort of business where other humans are involved in any way without special attention being given to thanking the customer. Even a good automated teller at a bank or savings and loan can say

Customers need
to be given special
care and thanked
for sharing their
hard-earned income
with our place
of business.

thank you, even if it only appears on the monitor screen. Thank you for doing business with us. It's recognition.

Stimulation and change is number two on the human want list—and another side of good management. A business should never be permitted to settle down into a well-worn groove of sameness. Even little changes can make a big difference. Change is a sign of life, of interest on the part of management. It shows management cares about the business and the customer, and security can be there too. Good service is a type of security, just as is a fine product and a refund policy. Customers need to be given special care and thanked for sharing their hard-earned income with our place of business.

Reminding employees is as important as initial training and regular inspection. It's so easy to fall back into bad habits. Customers should not wait to pay for their purchase, not a second longer than absolutely necessary. Restaurant customers should never have to sit and wait for their checks to be delivered to the table. Customers are not supposed to be waiters; don't make them wait.

For example, give them their bill before they're finished dining. Greet them with a smile at the cash register and thank them; really thank them by looking at them when they are paying their bill. Or if you take their payment at the table, tell them thank you when you return with their receipt. It makes customers feel important to you; and of course, they are important to you. They have the power to put you out of business if you don't give them the recognition they want. You have the power to make each transaction a success-building experience.

In any business, customers want you to recognize them; provide stimulating changes such as new items on the menu, fashion styles, décor, packaging, etc.; and security, including a quality product or service backed by value.

It's easy to treat customers the way we ourselves like to be treated. As the saying goes, never underestimate the customer. There are no unimportant customers, simply because there are no unimportant people. They want three things in this order: (1) *recognition* more than anything else in the world; (2) they want *stimulation or change;* and finally, (3) they want *security.* You can give them all three; and if you are wise, you'll never fail to give them all three.

Daily success opportunities are always presenting for those of us willing and eager to accept the risks and pay the price. Is it worth it? Of course, it's worth it. Make it a habit to put others first.

4

POSSIBILITY THINKING

"The great ideas that move us to be better and greater than we are now, are the deep anchors that will hold us steadfast in place when the great storms of life crash around us."

—Earl Nightingale

The common denominator of success is forming the habit of doing what most people don't like to do. And what most dislike most is making the wisest possible use of time—one act at a time all day long. Form this habit and as William James put it, you'll wake up one fine day to find you're among the competent ones of your generation.

Being one of the competent ones means we must be prepared. If doing things for a year seems like a big challenge, realize the people who rise to the top are people willing to do what the followers in life will not do.

Questions for your consideration: Are you as prepared as you should be? What do you know? How well have you

The common denominator of success is forming the habit of doing what others don't like to do.

developed whatever talents and abilities are inherent in you? Do you think the education you have is good enough to stretch over a lifetime? What are you doing about it? Are you a sponge soaking up knowledge on every side?

For many, a diploma or college degree is like a vaccination. In fact, it's called the Vaccination Theory of Education. These people believe that once the diploma or degrees are in hand, education for them is over. A college president reported that as he walked toward the podium on commencement day, he overheard a senior saying to another, "Thank God it's over. I'll never open another book as long as I live." He said they were the saddest words he ever heard.

Somehow the idea of education had not been sold to that young man, nor did he know the meaning, strangely enough, of the word "commencement." Education is a lifelong process and should end only when we do. And commencement means beginning, not end; beginning of independence, yes, but also the beginning of the enriching education that will hang the pictures in our minds and determine what we become as persons. Ideas.

The great ideas that move us to be better and greater than we are now, are the deep anchors that will hold us steadfast in place when the great storms of life crash around us. Many anchors prevent our being intimidated or diverted from our path by expediency or fad or shallow opportunity, and they provide us with a set of sensors that can pick up the dishonest and the phony.

Giving the cheap and shoddy, the quick buck, past a person conditioned by such ideas is like trying to sneak a sunrise by a rooster. Such great ideas provide a security system for us without disturbing our sense of humor. In fact, our sense of humor is greatly enriched by such ideas, and smiling and laughter become important parts of our days. Now we're by no means immune to mistakes but understand that they're a natural part of growth and reaching into the unknown future.

And are the ideas we hold in concert with our goals? They must be if our goals are to be successfully achieved. What is an idea? We say, "I have an idea." What is that? It's surely more than a neurochemical response, although it's that too. *An idea is the bringing together of known increments to provide a result.* "Let's go to the beach," someone says. Without a moment's hesitation, we take the "known" beach factor, add it to existing transportation, the proper clothing, possibly a picnic lunch, and suggest the resulting idea to those we're with at the time.

It all happens instantaneously, although all sorts of interconnections are going on in our brains. The greater our general information, the more combinations we can put together and the greater the reach of our "possibility thinking" as Dr. Robert Schuller calls it. That's why young people should think twice before complaining about school courses they'll never use as adults.

If you don't see opportunity in your work, you may not be looking deeply enough or creatively enough, so you don't see all the opportunities for expression available in your present work. Do you belong to the group that thinks education comes naturally just from being alive?

5

TOO GOOD TO BE TRUE

"Nothing is too good to be true."

—Earl Nightingale

We're all familiar with the expression, "It's too good to be true." We may even have used it ourselves from time to time. It's another of those self-defeating cliches that we can get rid of once and for all by examining what's too good to be true. What could be too good to be true? Nothing is too good to be true.

Another cliche worth getting rid of is the one that goes, "Well, you can't have everything." What in the world does that mean? You *can* have everything you need and seriously want. Most people do have everything they seriously want. What do you want very much and have wanted very much for any length of time that you don't have?

A very good friend of mine who used to be one of the principals of one of the country's largest and most successful advertising agencies (he's since passed away) used

Get rid of
self-defeating
cliches in your
thinking, speaking,
and writing.

to have an inflexible rule concerning anything turned out by his agency—no cliches. In fact, over the years, he had made a collection of cliches. He had hundreds of them and they were posted where all creative people could see them and avoid them.

There's even a book of cliches collected by Joseph W. Valentine. Cliches go back as far as recorded history. They tell us that: "All work and no play make Jack a dull boy." And that, "There's no fool like an old fool," "He's a chip off the old block," "a pretty kettle of fish," "That's the straw that breaks the camel's back," or "The straw at which a drowning man will clutch." "She has bats in the belfry," "His bark is worse than his bite," "Don't count your chickens before they're hatched," "Two heads are better than one," and on and on and on ad nauseum.

There are a few cliches, if any, that we would be much better off without. But it's like getting rid of a dog's fleas—either they multiply faster than you can kill them or they crop up later.

One of the worst cliches is, "You can't teach old dogs new tricks." This one is used mostly by people past the age of 40 or 50 who simply want to go on doing things the way they've always done them. People who resist changing with the times. But human beings are not dogs and knowledge is not a bag of tricks.

Whenever you find yourself about to repeat an old family cliche, you can put more interest into your conversation by substituting what you actually want to say instead of using a cliche. For example, instead of pulling out that tired threadbare bit about the old dogs and new tricks, you might say it's difficult to change long-established habits. Difficult, maybe. Impossible? Nonsense.

You'll find as I do that it's quite difficult not to use cliches. You may still say, "You're putting the cart before the horse," or, "Where there's smoke there's fire," or, "I think we're on the right track." There's really nothing wrong with using these venerable old sayings except that they're crutches we'd be better off without. Of course, we don't have to rush into this. After all, we don't want to "change horses in midstream," because we know that "haste makes waste." And since we've "made our beds, we'll just have to lie in them." But watch those cliches—don't let a well-worn phrase become truth or a habit.

If you decide to cut down on your use of cliches, get rid of these two cliches first: "That's too good to be true," and, "You can't have everything." Because nothing is too good to be true—and yes you can have everything.

6

THREE P'S AND AN F

*"Intelligence plus character—that
is the goal of true education."*

—Martin Luther King, Jr.

An education can give you four great objects of life:
poise, power, peace, and freedom. There are 10 marks of
an educated person: you can check them off to see how
you qualify as an educated person.

1. An educated person has an open mind—the
   ability to toss even your most cherished beliefs
   into the trash if you find they're not true.

2. You listen to all the information someone else
   can give on a subject and then draw your own
   conclusions.

3. You never laugh at new ideas—never say that
   something is impossible, ridiculous, or that it
   cannot be done.

4. You cross-examine your daydreams. A lot of people have become great by realizing that some daydreams can become practical realities.

5. An educated person discovers your strength and then makes the most of it, and each of us has one. Nothing succeeds like success, but mainly because a person has found his strong point and has learned how to use it.

6. You learn the value of good habits and how to form them.

7. You know when not to think and when to call in the expert to do your thinking for you.

8. An educated person doesn't believe in superstition. It's amazing and pitiable that a great number of people believe in lucky charms, certain days such as Friday the 13th, or signs such as breaking a mirror, black cats, and other irrational beliefs still around from the dark ages.

9. You live a forward-looking, outward-looking life. Psychology divides the world into two classes— introverts and extroverts. The inward-looking introvert loses health, efficiency, happiness, and so on—while the outward-looking person builds, constructs, organizes, achieves, and

harnesses the energies of the world. Most people are a combination of both introvert and extrovert, but it's important that we turn ourselves and our minds outward, not inward.

10. You cultivate a love for the beautiful. Beauty can be a fine book, good music, nature, a painting, any one of a million things. The educated person sees beauty in just about everything.

So those are the 10 marks of an educated person. How did you do? Pretty good? Great! You can "educate" yourself by building habits that result in being filled with poise (dignity and balance), power, peace, and freedom.

7

TRUTH VERSUS FEAR

*"Fear makes come true that
which one is afraid of."*

—Earl Nightingale

If fear of something is held long enough, it may well bring to us what we fear. But whether it becomes a reality or not, fear affects our mind and body as if the thing exists, doing inevitable damage to our physical bodies.

Some fear is perfectly natural—normal fears that work to keep us alive. But the annoying, unreasoning, illogical, and neurotic fear of something is because we don't know the real truth about it. When we know the truth, the fear vanishes. That includes a neurotic fear of death, the fear that we are not liked or loved, and so forth. Remember that when we fear something, it takes a toll on our mind and body just as if what we fear had in fact come to pass.

So how do we change an attitude of fear? My good friend, Dr. William Glasser, distinguished psychiatrist and

Ralph Waldo Emerson said that fear is ignorance.

author of *Reality Therapy* and *Schools Without Failure,* says if you want to change attitudes, start with a change in behavior. In other words, form a habit to act the part as well as you can of the person you would rather be, the person you most want to become. Gradually, the old fearful person will fade away.

Dr. Viktor Frankl, Nazi concentration camp prisoner, learned that by controlling his attitude, the suffering fell away. His mind was free to roam where he wanted it to roam. Think about what he wanted it to think about. It was as free as the birds, for his mind could fly to the ends of the earth to the ends of imagination in an instant—and so can yours.

All of this study of words and attitude goes back to my strangest secret. We become what we think about—consequently, habits can be broken. Deciding what you want to focus on is vital in becoming a powerful, competent thinker.

Processionary caterpillars traveled in long undulating lines, one creature behind the other. Jean-Henri Fabre, the French entomologist, once led a group of these caterpillars onto the rim of a large flower pot so that the leader of the procession found himself nose to tail with the last caterpillar in the procession, forming a circle without end or beginning.

Through sheer force of habit and, of course, instinct, the ring of caterpillars circled the flower pot for seven days and seven nights until they died from exhaustion and starvation. An ample supply of food was close at hand and plainly visible, but it was outside the range of the circle, so the caterpillars continued along the beaten path.

People often behave in a similar way. Habit patterns and ways of thinking become deeply established and it seems easier and more comforting to follow them than to cope with change—even when change may represent freedom and achievement.

If someone shouts "fire," it's almost automatic to blindly follow the crowd and many thousands have needlessly died because of it. How many stop to ask themselves: Is this really the best way out of here? So many people miss the boat because it's easier and more comforting to follow—to follow without questioning the qualifications of the people

Habit patterns and ways of thinking become deeply established and it seems easier and more comforting to follow them than to cope with change—even when change may represent freedom and achievement.

just ahead—than to do some independent thinking and checking.

It's hard for most of us to fully understand that people in such numbers can be so wrong, like the caterpillars going around and around the edge of the flower pot with life and food just a short distance away. If most people are living that way, it must be right, they think. But a little checking will reveal that throughout all of recorded history, the majority of humankind has an unbroken record of being wrong about most things, especially the important things.

8

PURE ENERGY AND CREATIVE POWER

"The idea is like the seed corn; it grows imperceptibly in secret."

—Johannes Brahms

All of us can, if we desire, tap an unsuspected source of pure energy and creative power. This source, fully adequate and freely available, is our silent partner—the subconscious mind. By correctly using this potential, we can gain release from tension and frustration and have at our disposal abundant energy and new mental power and physical well-being. These things we gain without striving. There's no laborious routine to follow. We simply recognize our subconscious mind and permit it to function under proper conditions.

When you observe the working habits of leaders in any field, you'll find that important discoveries are seldom made while engaged actively in research investigation.

The subconscious area of your mind is a bottomless reservoir of creative insight and intuition.

New insights, bold ideas and plans are contributed by the underlying activity of the mind, the subconscious function, and usually come during a time of leisure. Just about all great scientists, artists, writers, musicians, and top-flight businesspeople will tell you that their best ideas come not while they're actively engaged in seeking them, but frequently flash into their minds while engaged in other seemingly unrelated activities.

This is true of every really great man and woman who ever lived. For example, the most momentous concept of this age—the relationship of time and space and the nature of reality—sprang into the mind of Albert Einstein while he was confined to his bed because of illness. Who can say, but for this period of enforced quiet and relaxation, this world may not have been in the atomic age, good or bad, depending on your attitude.

The subconscious area of the mind is an unplumbed reservoir of creative insight and intuition. As high as 75 percent of scientists and inventors surveyed admitted that their best ideas did not come to them while they were actively engaged in work and research, but at odd moments when they were relaxing. Their discoveries were contributed by the inner underlying activity of the mind, the subconscious function.

You can put this tremendous problem-solving part of your mind to work with results you'll find to be amazing. You've probably noticed—just as do the great inventors, scientists, thinkers, artists, writers, and so on—that your best ideas come to you not when you're worrying about them or working at your desk or on the problem you're trying to solve, but rather your best ideas, the solutions to your problems, seem to just pop into your mind at odd times when you're relaxing, when you're not thinking of the problem. Of course, it wouldn't if you hadn't been thinking of it.

Have you ever tried to think of someone's name and the harder you thought about it, the more difficult it was to remember, but as soon as you quit thinking consciously about it, it popped into your mind? Well, this is your sub-conscious at work. It contains all information which has ever come your way. It stores every word, act, sight, smell, thought. Every conversation you've overheard, every sound, every book, paper, or magazine you've ever read. Add this fantastic storehouse of information to its natural intuition and you have a tool that can solve just about any problem you want to give it.

9

PLAYING THE ROLE

*"I created the character and then let
her play herself through me."*

—Shirley MacLaine

Have you ever thought much about the part you play,
your role in this great performance called life? Your role is
important. In fact, it may be far more important than you
realize. Nature has endowed many of our creatures with
what's known as protective coloring. The coloring of a
creature of the woods is such that it blends with the back-
ground, making it difficult to see. You can look right at a
motionless deer, elk, or bird, just about any animal and not
even see it because it so perfectly blends with its environment. The chameleon can even change color patterns to
blend with different backgrounds.

But as usual, nature gave to the human being an even
greater gift. We can make our surroundings match us. By
that I mean a person's environment will gradually change

By acting the part
of the person
we want to be,
we can gradually
actually become
that person; and
as we do, our
circumstances and
environment will
change to fit the
new personality.

to fit the kind of person he or she becomes, and that is where and how we act out our role on the stage of life, which becomes a matter of the greatest importance. It seems that before we can accomplish anything, we must first become the kind of individual to whom this something would belong.

By acting the part of the person we want to be, we can gradually actually become that person; and as we do, our circumstances and environment will change to fit the new personality—and each of us are the only creatures on earth who can bring about this wonderful and amazing condition.

Everyone knows that feelings trigger actions. That is, if you feel angry, you'll usually get angry. If you feel sad, you'll act sad. If you feel happy, you'll act happy. But what far too few people realize is that it will also work the other way around.

For example, let's say that you know the kind of person you'd like to be, that you're not completely happy and satisfied with the person you now are. If you have a clear mental image of the person you'd like to be, you can actually become that person in time by acting as though you were that person for a sufficient length of time—you make it a habit to think that way. You'll not only become that person in reality, but you'll also attract to yourself the kind of life and the things that person would have.

To the many who have discovered how wonderfully this little known information works, this will come as no surprise, but to most people it may be hard to believe. Sounds too easy. But actually, while it's true, it's not easy. It's not easy because it means getting rid of old habits and forming new ones, and at best, this is never an easy job.

You may find yourself slipping back into the old well-worn grooves of long-established habits, and you have to keep reminding yourself to get back on the track. Every time you go to do something, ask yourself how the person you want to become would do it. Every time something happens, before you automatically and habitually react in the old way, stop and ask yourself, *How would the person I want to become react to such a situation?*

Like an actor on the stage, you have to completely assume this new role, hour by hour, day after day, month after month. Most of us have a mental picture of the person we would most like to be. We can become that person completely. With work and conscientious effort and our surroundings, our environment will change accordingly.

10

DON'T UNDERESTIMATE YOURSELF

"It's wonderful what we can do if we're always doing."

—George Washington

Metaphors like "rain falls on everyone" or "the sun shines on everyone," have been used to illustrate that good ideas come in droves from the universe. And those who act on them become successful; the others do not. Most people who've had success will run into people who say, "That was my idea." The difference is that the person with initiative, who is motivated, acted on the idea. They took the risk. The spectators who claim it was their idea most likely did get the same inspiration. They just didn't take the next step.

Here's another metaphor: Opportunities are like time. Opportunities never stop presenting and the clock ticks the same for everyone. When you receive a spark of an idea, the key to success is not to underestimate yourself.

A successful life can belong to anyone who makes the attempt to explore their own deep reservoirs of talent and generally unused ability.

A woman asked me this question, "Isn't it better, Mr. Nightingale, for a person to realize their limitations?" My answer: "It's fine for a person to realize his or her limitations if they know what their limitations are."

Each of us knows that there are many fields in which we have little or no ability. But we should realize, at the same time, that there are fields in which we have not reached the limits of our ability, fields in which we will never reach the limits of our ability. The trouble with most people seems to be that they have a dwarfed and limited picture of themselves in their own minds; and as a result, they never really know what their true abilities are.

We marvel at the electronic brains humankind has invented and now uses in hundreds and thousands of applications such as problem-solving machines or guided missiles with built-in guidance systems that can cause them to dive into the middle of a small target thousands of miles away. These electronic creatures of the human mind and imagination have built-in success mechanisms. Once given a target, they'll successfully accomplish their missions.

The human brain is similar but a million times more complex, more miraculous, and more efficient than the finest electronic device or all of them put together. So then how can a person recognize his or her limitations when they will never, during their entire life, learn to utilize all of their potential?

If more people knew and understood that they have enormous possibilities that they habitually fail to use or even know they have, they'd do a lot more living. They'd know more, do more, have more in five years' time than they'd otherwise accomplish in a lifetime. The more I study this subject and the more the real experts in the field uncover, the more convinced I become that a successful life can belong to anyone who makes the attempt to explore his or her own deep reservoirs of talent and generally unused ability.

Examining your untapped abilities leads to understanding yourself, your habits, your power to succeed.

11

A BIG ENOUGH REASON

"Your world is a living expression of how you are using and have used your mind."

—Earl Nightingale

Psychologists have long determined that at least three out of four persons underestimate themselves in the areas of energy, ability, talent, and brains. But why do people underestimate themselves and, by doing so, miss out on the abundance they could know as a result of the greater contribution they could be making?

I think they miss out because of the simple fact that we all tend to discount the familiar. The stranger riding into town of Western fiction is always held in more awe and interest. He looms larger than old Charlie, the blacksmith, who was born and raised there. But the fact of the matter is that the stranger, Charlie, and the onlookers are all capable of greater effort and interest if they're given a big enough reason.

We give an inch
when we could be
giving a mile—and
then we wonder
why we travel
by inches instead
of by miles.

It's true that each of us has deep reservoirs of ability that we habitually fail to use. Why don't we use these great areas of sheer net profit for ourselves and the community? I think there are four reasons. They're not good reasons, but they are reasons all the same.

1. We don't *have* to use our talents or exert extra effort.

2. We're doing about as well as the next person.

3. We use averages as standards of satisfactory performance.

4. We don't know that we actually have so much reserve power and ability. We take ourselves for granted while we give more credit to other people.

We make our greatest mistake in failing to realize the entirely new worlds of gratification, service, and reward could be ours, would be ours if we lived more fully extended and closer to our potential. The tired old refrain we hear on every side is, "Why should I knock myself out?" Living closer to our potential means not knocking ourselves out at all. On the contrary, we'd find, perhaps for the first time, the great new world of mental and physical second wind that leads us to goals we hardly dared to dream of working, as most of us do in second gear.

We do what we want to do, in many cases, what we feel we have to do in order to slip by, but nothing more. We give an inch when we could be giving a mile—and then wonder why we travel by inches instead of by miles. You make yourself bigger, I think, by holding up a better mirror, a truer mirror that shows what you really could be. Then we see humanity for what it really is, a kind of convoy moving at a slow speed so as to protect its slowest member.

You should know that, as an individual, you can break loose from the convoy and chart your own course—and travel at your own speed.

12

THAT LITTLE VOICE

"The power which resides in him is new in nature, and none but he knows what that is, which he can do, nor does he know until he is tried."

—Emerson

How many times has some little voice within you told you to do or say something but you've not done it or said it because you weren't sure you could believe in yourself? How many times have you had an idea that seemed wonderful and you were for a moment filled with excitement and enthusiasm, yet you let it slip by because no one else was doing it or recommending it?

One of our greatest mistakes is in not trusting ourselves. You ought to read Emerson's great essay on self-reliance. To quote briefly from this timeless essay, he wrote:

> To believe your own thought, to believe that what is true for you in your private heart is true

Trust yourself to do what you know is right and true.

for all men—that is genius. ...A man should learn to detect and watch that gleam of light which flashes across his mind from within, more than the lust of the firmament of bards and sages.

Yet he dismisses without notice his thought, because it is his. In every work of genius, we recognize our own rejected thoughts: they come back to us with a certain alienated majesty. Great works of art have no more affecting lesson for us than this. They teach us to abide by our spontaneous impression with good-humored inflexibility then most when the whole cry of voices is on the other side.

Emerson goes on to write:

> There is a time in every man's education when he arrives at the conviction that envy is ignorance; that imitation is suicide; that he must take himself for better, for worse, as his portion; that though the wide universe is full of good, no kernel of nourishing corn can come to him, but through his toil, bestowed on that plot of ground which is given to him to till. The power which resides in him is new in nature, and none but he knows what that is, which he can do, nor does he know until he is tried.
>
> ...Trust thyself: every heart vibrates to that iron string. Accept the place the divine providence has found for you, the society of your contemporaries, the connection of events. Great men have always done so and confided themselves childlike to the genius of their age, betraying their perception that the absolutely trustworthy was seated at their heart, working through their hands, predominating in all their being. And we are now men, and must accept in the highest mind, the same transcendent destiny; and not minors and invalids in a protected corner, not cowards fleeing before a revolution, but guides, redeemers, and benefactors, obeying the Almighty effort, and advancing on Chaos and the Dark.

Emerson was not only one of the greatest thinkers in the world, he was also a truly great writer, and what he told us was to trust ourselves to do those things we know are right and true for us.

When something comes into your mind, and in that first fleeting instant if with all your being it's right and true for you, do it. Realize that in all the world, there's but one star for you as an individual to follow and follow it to your own destiny. Do not expect it to be the star of others for you. If you want a rich and rewarding life, remember Emerson's words that we should learn to detect and watch that gleam of light, which flashes across our mind from within, more than the luster of the firmament of bards and sages.

13

IDEAS

"Each of us has a tendency to underestimate our own abilities."

—Earl Nightingale

During this hour every day, I encourage you to take a completely blank sheet of paper and at the top of the page, write your present primary goal clearly, simply. Then, since our future depends on the way we handle our work, write down as many ideas as you can for improving what you now do. Try to think of 20 possible ways in which the activity that fills your day can be improved. You won't always get 20, but even one idea is good.

Now remember two important points with regard to this exercise—one, this is not particularly easy, and two, most of your ideas won't be any good. When I say it's not easy, I mean it's like starting any other habit. At first, your mind may be a little reluctant to be hauled up out of that old familiar bed; but as you think about your work and ways

Harness the power of your mind and take control of your goals.

it might be improved, write down every idea that pops into your head, no matter how absurd it might seem.

Let me tell you what will happen. Some of your ideas will be good and worth testing. The most important thing, however, that this extra hour accomplishes is that it deeply embeds your goal into your subconscious mind, starts the whole vital machinery working the first thing every morning. If you can come up with 20 ideas each day in that morning hour, that totals 100 a week, even skipping weekends. An hour a day, five days a week totals 260 hours a year, which still leaves you 3,740 hours of free leisure time. This means you'll be thinking about your goal and ways to improve your performance and increase your service more than six weeks a year—devoted to thinking and planning. Can you see how easy it is to rise above any so-called competition and still leave you with seven hours a day to spend as you please?

Starting each day thinking means that your mind will continue to work all day long. Then at odd moments when you least expect it, really great ideas will begin to bubble up from your subconscious. When they do, write them down as soon as you can. Just one great idea can completely revolutionize your work—and as a result, your life.

If you want to develop the muscles of your body, you exercise daily. The mind is developed in the same way, except that the returns are out of all conceivable proportion to the time and energy spent. The human mind can lift anything. Those muscles, even the best developed, are puny alongside those of some of the dumbest animals on earth.

If humans had to depend on their muscles for survival, they probably would've disappeared, as did the dinosaurs, which were incidentally the most physically powerful and most successful creatures that ever lived. This puts each of us in the driver's seat.

Let's briefly recap:

One, this week start spending one hour a day getting as many ideas as you can. Try for 20 ideas a day of ways to improve what you're now doing. Don't become discouraged. Remember the achievement of your goal very likely depends on this habit, as does your whole future. Once you start exercising your mind in this way, you'll want to continue the practice.

Two, if everything you now have is the result of using, say, 5 percent to 10 percent of your mental ability, you can imagine what life will be like if you can increase this figure to 20 percent or more.

Three, successful people are not people without problems. They're simply people who have learned to solve their problems.

Four, don't waste time and energy worrying about needless things. Forty percent of them will never happen. Thirty percent have already happened and can't be changed. Twelve percent are needless worries about health. Ten percent are petty miscellaneous worries. And only 8 percent are genuine. Try to separate the real from the unnecessary and solve those within your ability to solve.

Five, the human race has advanced further during the past 50 years than in all the preceding 10,000 years of human civilization. We're now living right in the middle of the golden age humanity has been dreaming of and praying for for centuries and it's going to get better.

Last of all, know that only your mind can take you to your goals in life. Use your mind effectively and follow through on the good ideas it supplies you.

14

FACT OR FANTASY

"We tend to become in real life exactly like the image we habitually hold of ourselves."

—Earl Nightingale

Scientists agree that the human nervous system is incapable of distinguishing between an actual experience and the same experience imagined vividly and in complete detail. That means that if you can imagine something very strongly, as far as your nervous system and its reactions, the event for all practical purposes has actually taken place.

The person who worries mentally, emotionally, and even physically projects into a situation that hasn't even occurred. In most instances, the person suffers as much or more than had the object of the worry actually taken place. Those who worry intensely about, say, failure of some kind find themselves experiencing the same reactions that accompany actual failure. Feelings of anxiety, inadequacy,

Your mind
and nervous
system form a
marvelous and
complex agency of
enormous power.

and humiliation, as well as the corresponding physical symptoms—headache and upset or painful stomach. As far as their mind and body are concerned, they have failed; and if they worry about it long enough, if they concentrate on failure hard enough, they will upset themselves to the extent that they will actually bring about the failure they dread.

While this coin has a destructive and painful side, it also has the reverse side. Using this inability on the part of the nervous system to distinguish between fact and fantasy, the imagination can be used to build a powerful and prevailing force for achievement and success. The mind and nervous system form a marvelous and complex agency of enormous power. They form an agency analogous to a computer in that they can only act on the data we feed into them.

People who worry about failure unwittingly defeat themselves. This same time and energy concentrating on the success they seek, a worthy goal toward which they can positively direct their efforts, marshals all their forces to work for them instead of against them. We therefore tend to become in real life exactly like the image we habitually hold of ourselves. This is why Lincoln was so right when he said people are about as happy as they make up their minds to be. They're also as successful or unsuccessful, and everything else, as they make up their minds to be.

Knowing this, it pays to evaluate our self-image from time to time:

- Will the image we hold of ourselves lead us to where we want to go and what we want to do?

- Is it a healthy, forward-momentum image?

- Is it an image of strength and accomplishment?

- Is it time to start building a more positive image of yourself?

If you think the image you have could stand some improvement, imagine that you are the central figure, the only figure for the most part in a motion picture that is to be used as a documentary of your life. In all of your acts—those that relate to the way you do your work and get along with others—how do you appear to the world? Act the part of the person you would most like your loved ones to see. As the central figure of such a film, you would most likely speak with more care, be more conscious of your appearance, have better posture, you would smile a great deal more, and probably be more thorough when you work.

Act the part of the person you would most like to be. Play the part as you would the lead in a play. And then one day the image you project to the world and the image you hold of yourself will be exactly what you want it to be.

15

DORMANT ENERGY

"Focusing on the life you want
releases your positive energy."

—Earl Nightingale

We are under an unspoken but enormous pressure to be average. Yet I wonder if you conducted a survey and asked 5,000 adults if it's their aim in life to be average, how many would reply yes? Would you? Would you be satisfied with an average education and an average income for the rest of your life?

Even though most people really don't want to be average, they have grooves of habit that they have spent 20 or more years forming that make them keep playing the world's most unrewarding game. The name of the game is "follow the follower." This is why as adults we should go back to that empty lot with a deeply worn path through it, using it as the symbol of our tendency to blindly follow without question. We need to plow it up, turn over every bit

Real desires
are definite,
concrete—and
create great energy
to accomplish
any goal.

of soil on that lot, and then smooth it out and build something on it more noteworthy than a path, or at least make a new path, an original path.

Of one thing we can be absolutely certain, if we follow anyone long enough, in the end we arrive at the place where the leader takes us. In some cases this might be great, but it's worth thinking about. It's worth checking their references. We should never make the mistake of thinking that because a great number, even a great majority of people are doing things a certain way that it's necessarily the best way. History just doesn't bear this out.

The pressure to be average and normal can have a major impact on your character and how you deal with others. What does being normal mean to your character? Visualization, focusing on the life you want, releases your positive energy.

People frequently say of someone, "I don't know where he gets his energy. He's going all the time." Have you ever wondered why some people seem to have more energy than others? Why some people seem to get so much done in so short a time? Well, I have the answer for you. The answer is *desire*. That's right. The amount of energy you use will always be in exact proportion to how much you want something.

I've heard it put this way: Perhaps you've been hoping to create energy in yourself. You can't create energy, either in yourself or elsewhere. Nobody can. You can only set energy free. Loosen it, transform it, direct it. An individual is born with a certain amount of energy. No more. And what is more important, you cannot put additional quantities into someone. You may sometimes seem to be putting energy into someone, but you're not. You're simply setting the person's original energy free, applying a match to the coal or fanning the fire.

Some individuals appear to lack energy when as a fact they're full of energy, which is merely dormant, waiting for the match or waiting for direction. The usual idea of the amount of energy possessed by an individual is the intensity of the desire of that individual.

Desire stimulates and uses energy. Strong, definite desires generally take more energy to fulfill. Without desires, energy is rendered futile. No one consumes energy in action unless they desire to perform the action, either for itself or as a means to a desired end. Don't confuse vague general aspirations with desire. Real desires are definite, concrete—and create great energy to accomplish any goal.

16

PERSONAL POWER

*"Your future is where you're going
to spend the rest of your life."*

—Earl Nightingale

Each of us has a natural tendency to think, act, talk, and conduct our lives the same way as the people who habitually surround us. So from time to time, we should ask ourselves, *Are the people I'm emulating going where I want to go? If I act like them, will I end up like them?*

This may be fine if the people are heading in the right direction, but at least you should be carefully and very objectively examining your associations from time to time. Now, the reason is clear. No two human beings are alike. We're all different, with different likes and dislikes, different talents and abilities. Take you, for instance—have you often thought of the fact that you're a marvelous, unique creature, the only one of your kind in the entire universe? I'm not saying this just to make you feel good; it's a proven scientific fact.

Your future is where you're going to spend the rest of your life.

So why should you follow anybody? You should have your own goals, your own schedule of work. You should have in your mind a clear picture of the kind of person you wish to become. If you subscribe to the truth that everything can be improved, and that improvement increases value, you'll realize that making improvements makes a lot of sense.

What would you like that future to be like? Are you going to decide for yourself or let other people decide for you? If you sit riding in the back of the wagon with your feet dragging, you have your back toward your future—where you go will depend upon the whims or desires of who is sitting up front driving the team. If that's okay with you, fine. But to me it seems like a big risk.

Maybe it's time for you to climb up on the seat and take those reins in your own hands. Maybe you don't want to go where the wagon's been heading in the past. This is a decision each of us must make at some time, or times, in our lives.

Just be sure you pick the right person to follow. We all have people in our past who've shaped us to be who we are today. Take time to evaluate the people who have influenced you in the past and who you want to impact your future.

If you patterned your life after a crook, you would become a crook too, wouldn't you? Sure you would. If you patterned your life after a minister, you'd become a minister. So here's the question you might ask yourself:

- After whom have I patterned my life?

- Are they people I want to be like?

- Are they going where I want to go?

- Do they live the way I really want to live?

- Are they in fact worthy of emulation?

- Can I take my one chance at life and make the most of it by following the people I've been following?

- Am I playing follow the leader or follow the follower—and just who is the leader in this big circle?

Well, here's an interesting experiment you can make on your own. You can go to virtually any neighborhood in any city in the country, and find people living in that neighborhood who live like each other, same kind of homes, yards, furniture, cars, front doors, picture windows, dogs, you name it. It gives the impression they were stamped on the same press and all came off the end of the same assembly line.

I'm not saying there's anything wrong with this necessarily, but it deserves some thought. The same thing applies to any neighborhood from the top to the bottom, makes no difference. We tend to conduct our lives as do those with whom we habitually associate.

Evaluate your associations and habits regularly; seriously consider all the people who influence your thoughts, lifestyle, relationships, future, etc.

17

THE STRENGTH OF MOTIVATION

*"Before you can do something,
you must be something."*

—Goethe

Many years ago, a famous Los Angeles restaurateur was asked by a newspaper reporter, "When did you become successful?" The restaurateur replied, "I was successful when I was dead broke. I knew what I wanted to do and I knew I'd do it. It was only a matter of time." He had a successful attitude long before the success he sought had become a reality.

But let me prove my point by giving you a test. If you conscientiously go about this test and concentrate on it every day, all sorts of wonderful things will begin happening in your life and it'll show you what a great attitude can mean.

So here's the test: Treat every person with whom you come in contact as the most important person on earth. And you do that for three excellent reasons:

"You don't pay love back. You pay it forward."

1. As far as every person is concerned, he or she is the most important person on earth.

2. Because that's the way human beings ought to treat each other.

3. By treating everyone this way, we begin to form an important habit. There's nothing in the world that men, women, and children want and need more than self-esteem.

Self-esteem is the feeling that they're important, that they're recognized, that they're needed, that they count and are respected. People will give their love, their respect, and their business to the person who fills this need, even if it's a short encounter.

Customers treated with excellent service become advocates for you. It's natural to share successes whether it's a good meal or a great sale. The term, "word of mouth advertising" sums it up. We tend to pay it forward. People *do* pass along experiences. That's why word of mouth advertising can also kill a business. "Pay it forward" is an expression for describing the beneficiary of a good deed and repaying it to others instead of the original benefactor.

Most will remember the term from a play in the movie, but the concept is really old. Some argue that the phrase may have been coined by Lily Hardy Hammond in her 1916 book *In the Garden of Delight.* She wrote, "You don't pay love back. You pay it forward." Making this principle a daily habit and practicing this concept requires a strong desire to serve others.

If I ask you to go out and run a mile, would you do it? Probably not. Would you run a mile starting right now if I offered you $5,000 in cash? How about $10,000? Would you run a mile if it would save the life of someone you love? So, yes, you would run a mile, wouldn't you? It all depends on one word—*motivation.*

Now, if someone offered you a salary of $100,000 a year after taxes, a hundred thousand a year, net and clear, to act as his company's representative in France, would you take it? There's just one catch—you have to learn to speak French in 90 days. Would you do it? If you wanted that $100,000 a year after taxes, you would. You'd spend the next 90 days studying as you've never studied before; and at the end of 90 days, you'd be speaking French quite handily. This is motivation. It simply means that what we do and how we do it depends upon the strength of our motivation, doesn't it?

18

YOUR STATE OF MIND

"I believe that some people maintain the best part of youth, which is its zest for life, its hope for the future, its interest in daily activities."

—Earl Nightingale

George Bernard Shaw said, "Youth is a wonderful thing. What a crime to waste it on children." I believe that some people maintain the best part of youth, which is its zest for life, its hope for the future, its interest in daily activities. It is true that youth is not a time of life, it is a state of mind. Again, the issues of life always come back to the fact that the way we use our minds determines what happens to us.

How do you habitually react to problems? The experts say there are four ways we can react to problems—two are positive, two are negative. You can check yourself on this:

- Number one is the direct approach, which is the most positive. People who take the

The quickest way
to see an issue or
problem dissolve
is to squarely
face it head-on.

direct approach just walk up to the front door of their problem and knock on the door. This is almost always the best approach.

- Number two is the indirect approach, which is the substitute or semi-positive approach. Instead of walking up to the problem and facing it squarely, people who use this indirect method try the side doors and windows. They use indirection, but it's still a positive approach to problems.

- Number three is the full retreat. These people just plain run away from their problems, and hope that while they're gone, the problems will disappear. This is a negative approach and solves nothing, the problems just keep piling up.

- Number four is the sour grapes approach in which the entire issue is avoided. These people view their desire, but don't even try, either by direction or indirection, to get it. They just say, "Well, I didn't want it very much, and anyhow, it's not much worth having." These are the people who seem to say, "I'm weak, helpless. Will someone please fix the world for me?" They hope that others will solve their problems for them.

You might think that a person's reaction depends on the problem, but experts say that people *habitually respond* pretty much the same way to all problems. The next time you go to a restaurant with a group, watch the way each person orders. You'll spot those who have never made their own decision. These people hem and haw and peek around the edge of the menu, waiting for someone else to make up their mind. They usually ask, "What are you going to have?" You answer, and still they ponder for a moment, then say, "Well, that sounds pretty good. I'll have the same."

Selecting a lunch or dinner from a menu doesn't sound very important, but it shows a habitual pattern. Another person will pay no attention to what the rest are ordering, but he can't make up his mind. He'll find two items that look good, and he just can't bring himself to sacrifice one in favor of the other. He really wants them both, and he's sick that he can't have them. Long after everyone else has ordered, he's still talking to himself and vacillating between the steak and the chicken. Once in a while, there is the person who looks down the menu once, picks the entry he wants, and puts the menu down to turn his attention to more important matters.

Usually, most of the others present (watch for this and see if it isn't true) will order as he did. Without even thinking about it, they're following someone who indicates, through his problem-solving attitude, that he's a leader. He has no interest whatsoever in what the others order. He knows what he wants, and that's that.

How do you stack up in this department? Do you knock on the front door, try to get into the windows or the back door, run away, or ask others to solve your problems for you? The experts point out that the quickest way to see a problem dissolve is to squarely face it before it has a chance to become magnified in the mind or marshal supporting forces.

19

WHEN PREPAREDNESS MEETS OPPORTUNITY

"Personal satisfaction and peace of mind comes only to the person willing to grow in value."

—Earl Nightingale

Preparation for life is so important. Success happens when preparedness meets opportunity. A great opportunity will only make the unprepared, the unqualified, appear ridiculous. Opportunities are all around you. Your ability to see them will depend in large part on how well you've prepared yourself. How do you stack up in this regard?

While this may sound elementary, you'd be amazed at the number of people who want more money but don't want to take the time and trouble to qualify for it. Until they qualify, there's no way on earth for them to earn it. This is like the person who wants a good-looking figure but doesn't want to change his or her eating habits.

If you don't like your income, you must devise ways and means of increasing your service. Your service must come out of you— your mind, your abilities, and your energy.

To nine-tenths of the world's population, the average North American is already rich. There's a greater difference between the standard of living of most of the world's population and our average worker than there is between the standard enjoyed by our average worker and the richest person in our society.

Our working people have just about everything the wealthiest have, only smaller. They have a home, car, often two of them. Radio, TV, savings account, debts, they're just smaller. Their food is as good and just as plentiful. Their beds are just as comfortable. Their home is just as warm in the winter. They have exactly the same amount of time and just as much, maybe more, freedom. Their life expectancy at birth is about 75 years; for the rest of the world on the average it's less than 60. With only a fraction of the world's population, we in the free world have half the world's total money income. We have more than two-thirds of all the automobiles on the planet.

So in talking about money, let's understand that we're already rich as a people. How much money do you need to live the way you want to live? To accomplish the goals you've established for yourself? Most people think they want more money than they really do. And they settle for a lot less than they could earn if they went about it the right way. The world will pay you exactly what you bargain for. Exactly what you earn, but not a penny more.

Do you remember that old poem that goes, "I bargained with life for a penny and life would pay no more"? Well, that's about it, we'll receive not what we idly wish for, but what we justly earn. Our rewards will always be in exact proportion to our service. If you don't like your income, you must devise ways and means of increasing your service. Your service must come out of you—your mind, your abilities, and your energy.

A strong person cannot make a weak person strong. But the power of you says that a weak person can become strong on his or her own by following a specific course of action for a sufficient length of time. A person who's already strong can become a lot stronger.

It's the same with this business of money. People who refuse to do more than they're being paid for will seldom be paid for more than they're doing. As mentioned previously, you may have heard someone say, "Why should I knock myself out for the money I'm getting?" This attitude more than anything else keeps people at the bottom of the economic pile. They don't understand that only as we grow in value as persons will we receive the increased income we seek. If we try to stand still in our work, and millions do, we'll never know the rewards or the joy of accomplishment.

Personal satisfaction and peace of mind come only to the person willing to grow in value, knowing that rewards are always in exact proportion to their service.

20

FORM THE HABIT

"Jot down your ideas, especially those that affect you emotionally, the ideas in which you want to personally become involved."

—Earl Nightingale

A good idea attracts money. The better the idea, the more money it attracts. Form the habit of using a legal pad and pen. Jot down your ideas, especially those that affect you emotionally, the ideas in which you want to personally become involved. An idea with no substance to it—nothing one can hold in his hands and rub against his brains—is just an idea, no more. Its value depends upon its implementation, the part that demands the rolling up of sleeves, the midnight oil, and the perspiration, but that's fun too when you're on the track of something big and worthwhile.

Talk about big ideas, there's no patent on the wheel. However, in the year 1911, patent number 1 million was reached and it had something to do with the old wheel.

Good ideas depend on implementation—rolling up sleeves, burning the midnight oil, and perspiring for as long as it takes.

Francis H. Holton of Ohio was granted patent number 1 million for a tack-proof pneumatic automobile tire. Technology has been the motivation for many inventors. There are experts who spend their time studying such things who believe we are rapidly, much more rapidly than most of us could possibly imagine, advancing toward such a future.

We are approaching the age of almost total leisure, an age in which perhaps 98 percent of our people will spend their time pursuing such things as pure education for education's sake, hobbies, sports, and other interests of all kinds. In this age of cybernetics, virtually all human functions as we know them today will be taken over by automation. Only about 2 percent of our population, they say, will produce all the goods and services needed. This 2 percent will consist of top management people in the various industries and the planners and scientists and technicians needed to keep the whole vast and complex machinery operating.

Our citizens can pursue any course that interests them. There will be writers, painters and sculptors, and others in the arts such as music and the theater, whose incomes will as always depend upon their popularity with the public. But in an age where 98 percent of the people do not work for a living, there'll be changes, almost too drastic for us to imagine today.

For one, just as today we have a minimum wage, in the age of cybernetics, the experts say that there will have to be a minimum income, whether a person chooses or can obtain gainful employment or not. This money will come back to their people through the profits earned by the businesses that supply their needs and wants.

Keep in mind here that I'm not advocating anything, I'm just reporting. I believe personally that the future will bring more employment opportunity than ever, not less. The experts go on to say that there will still be, of course, wide variations in income, but there will be a base income for every adult to live decently on minimums required for health and well-being.

21

THIS TIME IS THE RIGHT TIME

"Dig a little every day, that's the way."

—Earl Nightingale

One of the world's favorite alibis is that it's the wrong time to do something. When times are good, we don't have to do anything about them; and when they're bad, we say, "Well, the times are bad. So there's no use trying now." Here's an Emerson quotation worth remembering: "This time, like all times, is a very good one, if we but know what to do with it. I ask not for the great, the remote, the romantic. Give me insight into today, and you may have the antique and future worlds."

To the wise, the thinking person, today is always the right day for something. If there's a lack in one respect, there's always a corresponding opportunity in another. If times are bad, there are pressing needs because they're bad, and needs are opportunities. If times are good, then so much the better.

We're never more than
one good idea away
from great achievement
on any given day of
any week of the year—
if we form the habit
of looking on every
day and everything
in it with curiosity,
interest, and creation.

The opportunities are even greater, but the opportunities are always there. I read about a man who once bought a small railroad that had been losing money for years. He got it at a real bargain, but those who sold it to him secretly laughed at what they called his poor judgment. What they didn't know was that he was going to close the railroad, which he did, sold the rails and equipment at a good price and found himself with thousands of acres of real estate, which had formerly been right of way. The former owners had looked at it as a losing railroad. He looked at it as an opportunity to acquire valuable land.

Yes, this time, like all times, is a very good one, if we but know what to do with it. We're never more than one good idea away from great achievement on any given day of any week of the year, if we'll form the habit of looking upon every day and everything crowded into it with the eyes of curiosity, interest, and creation.

Every one of us is, at this moment, within reach of more opportunity than we could properly develop in our lifetime. And it makes little difference if you're selling something, or setting a broken leg, or doing the housework, driving your car, or just doing nothing at all. The trick to the whole thing is to *know the opportunity is there.* We'll look for something we know to exist in the area of our search, but most of the time we're not looking. We wait for someone else to find something before we suddenly become conscious that we're walking over buried treasure.

Then we dig frantically for a little while and then give it up again when nothing comes quickly to light. Instead, we should *dig a little every day*, realizing that since the treasure is definitely there, we'll eventually find our share of it because it most assuredly goes to the steady diggers, not the walkers, the idle talkers, or the occasional frantic diggers. Dig a little every day, that's the way. And know that every time is a good time because for every action, there's an equal and opposite reaction. What is bad carries with it a corresponding good, an opportunity that suddenly can be brought to light. This isn't Pollyanna. It's a fact recognized by thoughtful, successful people.

22

THE GENIUS OF UNHABITUAL THINKING

"Genius is little more than the faculty of perceiving in an unhabitual way."

—William James

The great William James and his principles of psychology define genius as little more than the faculty of perceiving in an unhabitual way. In his essay on habit, he referred to habit as the flywheel of society that keeps us doing what we've been doing in the past. Habit makes us fear change, regardless of the present condition of our lives. And the genius, as defined by Dr. James, seems to be that rare bird who knows that change is not only good but inevitable. The genius anticipates the inevitable and is perhaps what makes change inevitable. The genius habitually looks at everything in an unhabitual way and takes nothing for granted. The genius knows that whatever he sees that is man-made or served by man is imperfect and is always in the state of evolving.

Form the habit of seeing things not as they are, but as they perhaps will be, as they could be in the future.

Let me give you an example. A friend of mine was looking for a site for a large, luxury motel. He was in no hurry and spent months in a large West Coast city looking for the site that would probably best guarantee a good return on the really considerable amount of money he was going to invest and borrow. He found what, to him, was the perfect site. It was near a large university and at the confluence of five main roads, one of which was a heavily traveled highway. It was also within the city limits, which would mean a large local trade for the restaurant.

There was only one hitch. On the site was an old brick building, an old manufacturing concern still in business. He called on the owners of the business and told them what he wanted to do. Since that city had over the years grown around the old building, he pointed out that it would be to their benefit to sell him the property at a price many times the land's original value and build themselves a new, more modern plant in a less congested area.

They saw the sense of his plan and a way to pick up nearly half a million dollars for their property and close the deal. He razed the old building and built his beautiful new motel. Well, later, he discovered that many people in the motel business had looked upon that site as ideal for their purposes but had written it off because it was already occupied. But when my friend thought of the site, he saw not the old brick manufacturing, but instead saw his beautiful new motel sitting there. He had looked at that corner in an unhabitual way. By his genius, everybody benefited, including the community.

I think each of us can greatly increase the value of our life by taking to heart Dr. James' definition of genius by looking at things about us in our home and particularly in our work with new eyes, with the eyes of creation. We can form the habit of seeing things not as they are, but as they perhaps will be, as they could be, as our changing world will insist they be in the future.

Our lives are full of old brick buildings that have stood there for so long. We don't really see them anymore, or if we do, we just assume that they'll always be there. And maybe they always will if we don't do something about them. As someone has said—if you're still doing anything this year the same way you were doing it last year, you're behind the times.

23

UTILIZE YOUR RESOURCES

"There exists in each of us vast areas of untapped potential, nascent riches just waiting to be mined."

—Earl Nightingale

Studies show that people are happiest when they are busiest, and that people who look forward to the time when they can take it easy are likely to be disappointed and bored when they finally can. Being bored at the end of the day is not the result we want—and that won't happen if we remember the vast abundance of what we have.

The exciting course of our human history reveals discoveries and the development of natural resources. As far as we've gone—which isn't really very far when you consider how very young the human race is—we've done a pretty good job of developing the natural wealth that was here all along. We've harnessed electricity and tapped the deep

We can find quality and depth of life by forming the habit of looking within ourselves to narrow the gap between our former habitual way of doing things and our real potential.

pools of petroleum and tamed the atom. But there is today one largely unexplored area that contains more riches than all the wealth ever drawn from nature, and it is found in the area that exists between the human habitual way of performing and our potential.

Today's behavioral scientists put it this way. There exists in each of us vast areas of untapped potential, nascent riches just waiting to be mined. It seems that few people look within themselves for hidden wealth. They're accustomed to the habits they formed from childhood of acting like other people who as a rule are doing the same thing. Every so often they surprise themselves by discovering the ease with which they can solve their own problems on the rare occasions when they're forced to do so.

But for the most part we settle for moving along in low gear. Since there's always someone we can pass even in this gear, we draw satisfaction from this and find excuses for not moving at a brisker pace—for not forming positive momentum-building habits. It really isn't speed we want, it's quality and depth, and we can find it by forming the habit of looking within ourselves by consistently narrowing the gap that exists between our former habitual way of doing things and our real potential.

The idea seems to be to think of ourselves as having large unexplored areas of talent and abilities that are uniquely our own and each day try to bring more of them into play. A man running alone around the track will generally not run as fast as he will against competition. But there are people who become outstanding in their work because they are continually striving to do better. They're competing against themselves. They know that doing something the same way they've always done it isn't good enough, so each time they try to reach a little closer toward perfection.

When they're in the public eye as actors or musicians or performers of any kind, they come to be called great stars, in the sciences they're called geniuses, but their stardom and their genius is as Thomas Edison said, 95 percent perspiration. It takes time to mine the rich resources they have within themselves—and you can do the same.

There's a high school in Idaho with only 65 students. From that tiny student body the school music teacher has built a 35-piece band better than many schools with hundreds of students.

He simply developed more of what he had and everyone in the community is better off because of it. I heard the band the last time I was in Sun Valley, and like everyone else, I marveled that more than 50 percent of a school student body could be taught to play musical instruments well. That's utilizing your resources.

Yes, there is lurking within each of us the pathway to the abundance we seek in every facet of our lives. It's our job to find it, to keep searching until we've found our own individual way.

24

THE FUN OF LIFE

"I believe this unhappiness to be very largely due to mistaken views of the world, mistaken ethics, mistaken habits of life leading to destruction of that natural zest and appetite for possible things upon which all happiness, whether of men or animals ultimately depends."

—Bertrand Russell,
The Conquest of Happiness

Who do you think is the most fortunate? The person who inherits wealth or the person who must earn whatever wealth he'll ever have with his own brains and hands? Well, in my opinion, although I don't think I'd have said this 20 years ago, it's the person who is forced to make his own way in the world.

A good friend of mine is an executive with a large national corporation. He earns a very large income. While he has the

Happiness is not a result of what happens to us, but rather the cause of what happens to us.

good sense to save part of all he earns for the safety and protection of his wife and children and for his own eventual retirement, he has made it a point to tell his children that he's not going to leave them a dime, not one red cent. What's more? He means it, and his children know he means it—and his children love him very much for the kind of man he is, not for what he might leave them someday.

There's nothing wrong with a man leaving a lot of money to his children. If a man has a lot of money and he wants to leave it to them, it's his business what he does with the money he earns. I'm just saying that in my opinion it's best to be on one's own, to make the grade in life with our own brains, talents, and abilities just as our fathers and their fathers before them did. There have been numerous cases of young men taking over their father's companies and doing outstanding jobs in many cases, much better than the fathers might have done. These young people have shouldered their responsibilities and kept the family business going and in the family and they're to be congratulated. It wasn't their fault they were left a lot of money and a business to operate, but I do believe they get cheated out of a lot of the fun of life.

I think it's best to stand at the starting line with nothing more than youth, strength, ambition, and determination, and then the game begins. If a young man is wise, he'll first make it his business to learn the rules. Playing any game before you've carefully studied the rules will usually lead to losing. If you try to learn the rules by trial and error, you're taking a chance that you may run out of time before you've learned how to win. You're also overlooking the wisdom of the men and women who have played the same game for centuries and have left the rules clearly written in books for you to read. So the young person who really wants to win at this most exciting of games will make it their business to get the kind of education that is commensurate with the size of their goals. With the rules firmly in mind and followed every day, anyone can win.

You are in the act of winning. All you must do to win is decide upon the point you want to reach and reach it. Then if there's still time, you can play the game again and still again. Each time it's easier, since the rules by this time have been shaped into habit and you do the right things automatically, just like you get dressed in the morning and drive a car. Then having won, you can take your rewards with joy and satisfaction knowing that you played your own game and played it well.

Sidney Harris wrote in the *Chicago Daily News*, "The most miserable people I have known have not been those who suffered from catastrophes, which they could blame on fate or accident, but those who had everything they wanted except the power to enjoy it."

Have you noticed how true that is? That's why it's silly to say, "I'd be happy if such and such happened." Either we are happy or we aren't. And if we're not happy, we have formed habits that lead to general boredom or unhappiness. And these habits generally keep people down regardless of what happens.

Some people seem to be born with the knack for being happy and they're happy all the years of their lives. These are the truly fortunate people, like those who are born with an unusual talent of some kind. If we say we don't belong to the happy group, we can through study and concentration learn to be happy. The first thing we need to realize, I think, is that happiness is an inner comprehension like charm or good manners. It's not a result of what happens to us but rather is the cause of what happens to us.

25

"THAT'S GOOD"

"Success is not final, failure is not fatal: it is the courage to continue that counts."

—Winston Churchill

Our good friend, W. Clement Stone, one of this country's wealthiest and most successful business leaders, formed a habit in the early days of his career saying, "That's good." Whenever anything happened, good or bad. Most of the time, of course, it was something good.

But even when he learned of a near calamity, a deadly serious situation that would've sent a lesser man scurrying for cover, he'd smile and say, "That's good." Then as his associates shook their heads in resigned disbelief, he'd tear headlong into the problem and find what was good in it. Invariably, some element in the situation could be turned to advantage.

Of course, there are times when misfortunes come down on all of us in bunches like bananas. Yet if we

Something good can usually be found in almost any situation.

understand that something good can usually be found in almost any situation, we'll go quietly and efficiently to work on the most important part of the problem, the one that can be turned to advantage. When that's taken care of, we can go on to the next part. That's the best thing we can do, and it's the realistic way to get rid of discouragement before it gets rid of us.

Everyone has days or even successions of days when nothing seems to go right. A large account is suddenly lost. Anticipated plans fall through. It seems as though the sun has gone out. This is the time to take the long-range intelligent view. Since self-pity or inactivity cannot possibly help the situation, the only rational course to follow is to go after another large account, to make more presentations, replace those lost sales, to be confident in the knowledge that over the long haul things will average out to our advantage.

But even more important, losing an account, being disappointed, or failing to convince others on some point important to us often gives us just the pause we need to ask ourselves, "Why?" Maybe we're doing something wrong. Maybe something we're doing, while it isn't exactly wrong, could be done better. Here's an opportunity to improve ourselves and possibly increase our effectiveness in dealing with others. Some of the most successful people I know have at one time or another been forced by a stretch of poor productivity to analyze their methods and use of time.

A dry spell is no fun for anyone, but it's often the only situation extreme enough to get us to look at ourselves, find out what we're doing, why we're doing it, and whether this is the best possible way it can be done. As Emerson said, when a man is pushed, tormented, defeated, he has a chance to learn something.

26

LIFE'S LUSTER

"One of the most common mistakes we make is to let the luster fade from our lives."

—Earl Nightingale

Have you ever thought much about newness? It's the quality people are talking about when they say, "A new broom sweeps clean," or, "Turn over a new leaf." Well, newness, like most things, has its good side and its bad depending on how we look at it. A person in the new job, for instance, may feel he's at a disadvantage. He may be nervous, uncertain of just what he's supposed to do or how to do it. Sometimes he's bewildered by all that's going on around him. Maybe he's even a little scared, but even so, the person who's new to a business has a unique advantage over some of the other more seasoned men in his company. His job has a sparkle about it. There's a luster, a challenge in a new job that isn't always present once the position becomes familiar.

Maintain your enthusiasm and luster in life by seeing your product or service through the eyes of your happy customers.

Do you remember your first day at work? I do. I can remember the first time I sat down in front of a microphone as though it were yesterday instead of a good many years ago. Even though it was a small radio station—so small I used an old walk-in refrigerator as a studio—to me, it was one of the most exciting days of my life. I was scared and nervous, and I sounded like a man with his neck caught in a car door, but I was thrilled too.

How about your job? Does it still hold the excitement it did on that first day? It should, and it can, but does it? One of the most common mistakes we make is to let the luster fade from our lives. As it does, we gradually lose our enthusiasm, and if we're not careful, we'll settle down into a worn, tired groove of dull, uninteresting habit. We become like oxen yoked to a mill, going around in circles with our eyes fixed only on the worn path of our feet.

People who allow themselves to get in a rut usually don't realize that a rut is little more than a grave with both ends knocked out. So how can we stay out of this deadly rut? How can we keep our enthusiasm and maintain the luster in our lives instead of allowing it to fade with time and familiarity? The answer lies in reminding ourselves of things we already know but sometimes tend to forget.

A Chicago executive once told me how he maintained a luster in his job, how he charged his batteries during the early days of his career. Whenever overfamiliarity with his product and service or the negativism of some of his prospects or associates began to undermine his enthusiasm for what he was selling, he simply made a service call on one of his best customers. There he could reassure himself of the excellent results being realized through the use of his company's products. Then my friend would head out again with renewed confidence in himself, in his ability to be of service, and in the benefits he could deliver to every new prospect.

Even though the everyday details of our work may seem old hat to us, we should remember that those we serve look forward eagerly to the product or service. A person may be indifferent about many things, but the things we spend our money for aren't among them. We shouldn't be indifferent either, and we won't be if we'll look at our own product or service through the eyes of a happy customer.

People are on stage every day. Like the actors in a Broadway play, they're sometimes required to say the same words and go through the same basic actions day after day and week after week. The professional actor learns his lines and movements and then performs the part every day, often twice a day for as long as the play can run. Actors can never allow themselves to become bored with the role any more than we can afford to become bored with our work. The actor knows the audience is a new one for every performance. What the actors do isn't boring to them.

27

MONEY AND HUMAN NATURE

"The way to wealth is as plain as the way to market. Waste neither time nor money but make the best use of both."

—Ben Franklin

Did you ever hear the old fable about the man who was riding across the desert at night, and as he was crossing a dry river bed, a voice came out of the darkness ordering him to halt. The voice then said, "Now get off your horse," or camel or whatever it was he was riding, and the man got off. And the voice said, "Pick up some gravel from the riverbed." Well, the man did and then the voice said, "Now mount and ride on. In the morning, you'll be both glad and sorry." Well, when it became light enough, the rider looked at what he had picked up in the riverbed and discovered it wasn't gravel at all. It was a handful of precious gems. And as the voice had said, he was both glad and sorry. Glad he had picked up a few and sorry he hadn't picked up more.

Well, like most fables, this one is based on human nature and I guess it's particularly true in the United States of America. I think we all realize that we're living in the richest country the world has ever known. As a matter of fact, we're right in the middle of the golden era that humans have dreamed of and hoped for since the days of Pythagoras, Plato, and Aristotle. American workers, compared to the incomes earned in most countries, are a wealthy group. Compare their income and standard of living to even Americans of 50 years ago, and we are regular tycoons.

But most modern American families are like the man in the fable who picked up a few precious stones thinking they were gravel. They're glad to have such a high standard of living, but about 95 percent of them wind up sorry, because they never woke up to the fact that financial independence has nothing at all to do with the money they're paid—it has to do only with the money they save.

Out of 100 young American men who all start even at age 25, 40 years later when they would be 65, only one out of the original 100 is well-to-do. Four are financially independent for life, and the rest, the 95 percent, didn't make it. Now this wouldn't sound so bad maybe in some famine-ridden, undernourished, and depressed country, but this terrible situation is going on right here in the richest country on earth. It's a little-known fact that regardless of what a person happens to do for a living, they can be financially independent for life by age 65 if they only give a dime out of every dollar to the forgotten man, himself, and the forgotten family, his own.

Here's an interesting little test. Take the number of years you've been married times your income times 10 percent. That's how much you should have in a permanent never-touched savings program for your later years. If it comes out right or better, you belong to the top 5 percent of the people in this country. If it's less, you're in the 95 percent boat, and this is not a good boat to be in. As cited at the beginning of this segment, Ben Franklin declared many years ago, "The way to wealth is as plain as the way to market. Waste neither time nor money but make the best use of both."

We all want more and we're all sorry for not having enough. People have fought and argued over the concept that money is somehow bad. A misinterpreted Bible verse has caused many to proclaim the evils of money, when that verse in fact states it's the "love of money that is the root of all evil," *love* being the operative word. Many of those who like to throw around the concept that money is bad and being poor is good are preachers themselves. Well, those preachers should also look up a verse in 1 Timothy 6:5 that says, "Clearly, they think religion is a way to become rich."

Money is as good as the people who manage it. There's another verse that paraphrased says, "Use worldly wealth to gain friends for yourselves. If you have not been trust-worthy in handling worldly wealth, who will trust you with

Money is as good
as the people
who manage it.

true riches? If you have not been trustworthy with someone else's property, who will give you property of your own?"

C.S. Lewis, who at one time in his youth was an atheist, but later a best-selling author on his renewed faith, had something to say about the love of money. In *Perelandra,* the second book of his Space Trilogy, he wrote, "Was it possibly the root of all evil? No. Of course, the love of money was called that, but money itself? Perhaps one valued it chiefly as a defense against chance, a security for being able to have things over and over again."

Millions seem to believe that it's wrong to deliberately set out to earn a lot of money. It's not at all wrong. A sound economic base is a prerequisite for nearly everything we want to do. It also means we're serving people. Money is a fact-of-life resource. The more we have, the more we can do with it. The people with money can do most for those without it. Poor people tend to serve little, and since their sowing is limited, so is their harvest. But by far the great majority of unsuccessful people are unsuccessful because of the limited nature of their information base, their education on this subject. Now this doesn't mean they're uneducated on other subjects. They may well be. But if they don't know what produces enough money to live well, they will remain unsuccessful in the money department. That doesn't mean they'll be unsuccessful people by any means.

Some of the most successful men and women never earn very much money, but successful people tend to produce the wherewithal they need from one source or another. Millions stop growing at a certain stage of their development, some at 17, others at 19 or 20, and millions at 30 or 35. And from that point onward, they coast, making little or no effort toward self-improvement. Perhaps the most astonishing fact of all is the way people try to stretch an education, which for most of them ended at about age 18, and for those who went to college, at 20 or 21. They take what is at best a very rudimentary education, then try to stretch it over an entire lifetime. This renders them woefully inadequate to properly cope with life's problems, and just as important, to fully take advantage of a long life's opportunities.

28

THE WAY TO REALLY LIVE

*"When you increase the number of tasks
and perform them all efficiently, you are
establishing the habit of success."*

—Earl Nightingale

Each day consists of a series of tasks, tasks of all kinds, and the success of the day depends upon the successful completion of most of these tasks. Now if everything we do during the day is a success, that is done in the best fashion possible, we can fall asleep that night in the comfortable knowledge that we've done our very best, that our day has been a success, that one more stone has been successfully put into place. Now this is the way to really live.

Do each day all that can be done that day. You don't need to overwork or to rush blindly into your work, trying to do the greatest possible number of things in the shortest possible time. Don't try to do tomorrow's or next week's work today. It's not so much the number of things you do,

It's not the number of things you do, but the quality, the efficiency of each separate action that counts— the quality of what you do.

but the quality, the efficiency of each separate action that counts—the quality of what you do.

Gradually, you'll find yourself increasing the number of tasks and performing them all much more efficiently. Then you are establishing the habit of success. And that's why successful people go from one success to another because it's a habit with them. To form the habit of success, you need only to succeed in the small tasks of each day. This makes a successful day. Enough of these and you have a successful week, month, year, and lifetime.

This is why I say success is not a matter of luck. Far from it. It can be predicted and guaranteed, and anyone can achieve it by following this plan. Almost before you realize, you'll have achieved your goal. In looking back, you'll realize that your success was not attributable to any one day, week, or month, but rather it was the consistent, unrelenting, successful succession of single days that turned the trick. This is the way a skyscraper, a home, or a human life is successfully built, one successful day at a time and each day comprising a collection of successful tasks, one successful task at a time.

In order to advance to the place you've chosen, two things are necessary: one, keep your eye on your goal; and two, continue to grow from the standpoint of competence and effectiveness. Don't get impatient. Don't let the hundreds of little distractions each day try to get you off course, to bother you. Pay no attention to them, shake them off and stay steadily on the track. Concentrate on

Your success will not be attributable to any one day, week, or month, but rather it was the consistent, unrelenting, successful succession of single days.

each task of the day from morning to night and do each as successfully as you can. Know full well that if each of your tasks is performed successfully or at least the greater majority of them, your life will be successful. There's no other option. There's no way to avoid it.

29

CREATIVE THINKING

"The world of reality has its bounds; the world of imagination is boundless."

—Rousseau

Out of bad habits, people cling to an idea as though it's the best, if not the only idea they'll ever get. And are we anticipating the future when creating or building something new? A good example of foresight is found in the main streets of towns and cities built by the Mormons when they moved West. They were riding horses and driving wagons then, but they built broad, beautiful streets that easily accommodate the heavy automobile traffic of today.

Rather than forming momentum-building new habits, we tend to cling too long to past successes, systems, and methods. If a process is working well today, think about it with the future in mind. We're seeing an accelerating rate of change unprecedented in history; and because so many

Creative thinking, or selling, is an art, and can be mastered in time through regular practice of basic principles so you can use them to your advantage every day in your personal life as well as in your profession.

businesses are still living in the past, there are yawning opportunities on practically every side.

How many businesses in your town haven't made a single change in 20 years? In some cases, that may work. For example, a fine old restaurant that's perhaps better now than ever because of its age and strict adherence to quality—but the businesspeople of a community owe it to their customers and the community to keep abreast of current and future excellence, to put part of their profits back into the business to accommodate changing times and tastes.

Each honest calling, each walk of life has its own elite, its own aristocracy based on excellence of performance, and that applies to every field of human endeavor. We can develop habits of excellence in everything we do. We need to think in terms of excellence. We should demand it in what we buy and produce it in what we do.

It's well known that everyone has imagination, creative potential. We are born with these attributes, but some people never fully realize the value of their imagination and seldom put it to work. Persuasion can and should be one of our most creative pursuits, and it will be if we choose to make it so. Creative thinking, or selling, is an art, and can be mastered in time through regular practice of basic principles so you can use them to your advantage every day in your personal life as well as in your profession.

Writing instruments are among the most basic tools for creative thinking. I have a friend who keeps a pencil and a small pad of paper on the shelf next to his bathroom mirror.

He tells me that some of his best ideas come to him during the morning rush when his face is half covered with lather. Ideas are like slippery fish. They can strike at any time, and if we don't draft them at the point of a pencil, they're liable to get away.

Dorothea Brande, outstanding editor and writer, discovered creative thinking for herself and tells about it in her fine book *Wake Up and Live!* Her entire philosophy is reduced to the words, "Act as though it were impossible to fail." She tested herself with sincerity and faith, and her entire life was changed to one of overwhelming success.

I suggest you test yourself with this philosophy for 30 full days. Don't start your test until you've made up your mind to stick with it. By being persistent you demonstrate faith. Persistence is simply another word for faith. If you don't have faith, you will never persist. If you should fail during your first 30 days, by that I mean suddenly find yourself overwhelmed by negative thoughts, start over again from that point and go 30 more days. Gradually your new habit will form until you find yourself one of the wonderful minority to whom virtually nothing is impossible.

Believe in yourself—the power of you is exciting and perhaps a bit overwhelming, but this positive habitual mindset will launch you into daily success that you will experience in a variety of ways.

30

EXCELLENCE

"Excellence is an art won by training and habitation. We do not act rightly because we have virtue or excellence, but we rather have those because we've acted rightly. We are what we repeatedly do. Excellence then is not an act, but a habit."

—Aristotle

The person who writes a daily column for the newspapers, the cartoonist with a daily syndicated feature, or perhaps the Hollywood script writer on a definite assignment sooner or later draws a blank. That is, with a deadline approaching, a deadline that must be met, the writer is without a single idea.

You put a piece of paper in the typewriter and then stare at it. You let your mind wander. You concentrate. You dance around your library. You read something. Then you begin to think of all the things you'd rather be doing. Fishing, maybe,

Success is a matter of forming the right habits, and the best way to form the right habits is to do something you know you should be doing every day.

or playing golf, or traveling to some distant place—and then you forcibly bring your mind back to the job at hand and start the whole thing all over again. There's the typewriter with a blank white sheet in it, and there's the approaching deadline. Do you know what you do? You begin to write. You just begin.

This is why the professional writer laughs when he or she hears someone say, "I have to wait for the mood," or, "I must court the muse and wait for inspiration." The men and women who earn their living writing against deadlines would starve, or find some other business if they waited for inspiration.

One time some years ago, I spoke before a university journalism class, and one of the comments I made was later to come back and haunt me. I told them that if they were really serious about writing, writing for a living, they should write something every day, even if it was nothing more than making a few notes on the back of an envelope. Write something every day. And if they found they couldn't think of anything to write, to write anyway. I still believe I was right, but there have been many times when I've sat and stared at a blank sheet of paper for four or five hours before I could even write or think of a single word.

Success as a writer is the same as in any other field. It's a matter of forming the right habits, and the best way to form the right habits is to do something you know you should be doing every day. The more you do it, the easier it becomes, the more competent and confident you become, and the work becomes steadily better.

Also, the more you do, the more ideas you get for future work. I guess we all know that the longer you put off what you know very well you should be doing, the more you dread doing it. Finally, because of our procrastination, the job looms far larger than it did in the beginning, until we finally, in a kind of wild desperation, pitch into it and discover that it really wasn't nearly as bad as we thought it was going to be, and we should have done it at once, in the beginning, without wasting all that time storing up all that apprehension and being miserable sidestepping our responsibilities.

I'm willing to make a guess right now that you have something you should have done days or maybe even weeks ago, but you've been putting it off, hoping it'll go away. If you don't mind taking some advice from a person who makes it a practice to procrastinate, do your something now. Just pitch in and start. Before you know it, it'll be finished.

To become a writer or any other profession, here's another quote that you'll need: "What looks like the end of the road is really only a bend in the road." Don't look at the sudden loss of a habit or a way of life as the end of the road. See it instead as only a bend in the road that will open up all sorts of interesting possibilities and new experiences. After all, you've seen the scenery on the old road for so long, and you obviously no longer like it.

The breaking of a long-held habit does seem like the end of the road at the time, the complete cessation of enjoyment. Suddenly dropping the habit so fills our minds with a desire for the old habitual way that for a while, it seems there will no longer be any peace or any sort of enjoyment in life. But that's not true.

New habits form in a surprisingly short time, and a whole new world opens up to us. For those who have tried repeatedly to break a habit of some kind only to repeatedly fail, falling is not failing unless you fail to get up. Most people who finally win the battle over a habit they've wanted to change have done so only after repeated failures, and it's the same with most things. So don't think of it as the end of the road, but as a bend in the road, and falling is not failing unless you fail to get up again.

ABOUT EARL NIGHTINGALE

Earl Nightingale (1921-1989) was a man of many talents and interests—nationally syndicated radio personality, entrepreneur, philosopher, US Marine, and more. One thread united all his pursuits—a passion for excellence and living a meaningful existence.

Earl Nightingale's life began simply. He grew up in Long Beach, California. His parents had little money, and his father disappeared when he was 12. But even as a boy, Earl was always asking questions, always reading books in the local public library, wanting to understand the way life works.

Stationed aboard the battleship USS Arizona, Earl Nightingale was one of a handful of survivors when that ship was destroyed and sank at Pearl Harbor. After being separated from the Marine Corps and starting with practically nothing, over the next ten years he founded and headed four corporations. In addition, he wrote, sold, and produced 15 radio and television programs per week.

Nightingale appeared on all major radio networks. For four years he was the star of the dramatic series *Sky King,* which was carried on more than 500 stations of the Mutual Radio Network. He also began an insurance agency, and in twelve months led it from last to sixth place in the nation with one of the world's largest companies.

The Nation's Press carried the astounding story of the phenomenally successful young man who, at 35, had become financially independent. He produced his famous recording of *The Strangest Secret,* revealing how anyone can make the most of his or her own capabilities and can attain a rich full measure of success and happiness, right in his or her present job or position. Its theme: "How to achieve greater success and enjoy greater happiness and peace of mind."

At the time, this inspiring recording broke sales records, selling in the multimillions to major industries, retailers and salespeople, clubs and associations, parents, students, and people in virtually all walks of life. His masterful recording has been adapted into books and videos.

 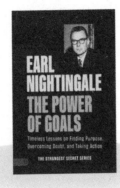 

THANK YOU FOR READING THIS BOOK!

If you found any of the information helpful, please take a few minutes and leave a review on the bookselling platform of your choice.

BONUS GIFT!

Don't forget to sign up to try our newsletter and grab your free personal development ebook here:

soundwisdom.com/classics